PREACHING IN THE
HOLY SPIRIT

PREACHING IN THE
HOLY SPIRIT

ALBERT N. MARTIN

Reformation Heritage Books
Grand Rapids, Michigan

Preaching in the Holy Spirit
© 2011 by Reformation Heritage Books

Published by
Reformation Heritage Books
2965 Leonard St., NE
Grand Rapids, MI 49525
616-977-0889 / Fax: 616-285-3246
e-mail: orders@heritagebooks.org
website: www.heritagebooks.org

Library of Congress Cataloging-in-Publication Data

Martin, Albert N.
  Preaching in the Holy Spirit / Albert N. Martin.
      p. cm.
  ISBN 978-1-60178-119-2 (pbk. : alk. paper) 1. Preaching.
2. Holy Spirit. I. Title.
  BV4211.3.M26 2011
  251—dc22
                                        2010049369

---

*For additional Reformed literature, both new and used, request a
free book list from Reformation Heritage Books at the above address.*

Contents

Preface

It was a Thursday night in February of 1952, and I was approaching my eighteenth birthday. I left my house to walk the one-and-a-half miles to the main business area in the town of Stamford, Connecticut. In those days all the stores remained open until 9:00 p.m. on Thursdays. I knew that many of my high school buddies would be hanging around ("chilling out") in front of the Liggette's Drug Store on the main street. That spot was the place where I and several other recently converted young people were scheduled to meet and conduct our first open-air street meeting. Several old white-haired men of God who had been brought into our lives urged us to venture forth with our newfound faith in this way.

After lustily singing several hymns and choruses, the time came for me to step forward in that little semicircle of young people in order to give my testimony and to preach the gospel. With my recently acquired leather-bound New Testament with Psalms in hand, I stepped forward, opened my mouth, and began to speak. Much to my surprise, although I was a natively timid and fearful young man, I was made conscious of the presence of dynamics that profoundly influenced what I said and how I said it on that memorable night. In a real sense, that night was my "coming-out party" in openly and boldly confessing my attachment to Christ before my peers. It was also my "spoiled-for-life party," in that I experienced on that occasion what I now know to be the immediate agency and operations of the Holy Spirit in the act of preaching.

Now, fast-forward fifty years. It is October 2002. The place is no longer a street corner but the auditorium of Trinity Baptist Church in Montville, New Jersey. The occasion is the annual pastors' conference held each October in the church. In that setting I was privileged to preach two messages on the subject "Preaching in the Spirit." Those messages were the ripened fruit of fifty years of scriptural investigation, constant study, and observation relative to this vital subject of what is involved in preaching in the Spirit. God was gracious in drawing near to us with a heightened sense of His presence as I delivered those two messages. A spirit of deep brokenness descended upon the men. Several mature men urged me to commit the substance of those sermons to the more accessible and permanent medium of the written page. And now...you know the rest of the story. You are holding it in your hands.

I commend these pages to God for His blessings with the prayer that because the substance of those two sermons is now embalmed in printer's ink, there may be more preaching "with the Holy Ghost sent down from heaven" (1 Peter 1:12).

November 2010   Albert N. Martin

CHAPTER 1

❧

The Agency and Operations
of the Spirit in Preaching

To penetrate more deeply into my special concern on this topic, consider this expanded title in a style typical of the Puritans: "The Immediate Agency and Operations of the Holy Spirit in and on the Preacher in the Act of Preaching." Two introductory matters will ease us into this vital theme: first, an exegesis of the language of my longer "Puritan" title; and second, an identification of several crucial presuppositions relative to the person and ministry of the Holy Spirit in general. Having accomplished that, we will focus on the person and ministry of the Holy Spirit in and on the preacher himself in the act of preaching.

Defining the Topic
First, what do I mean by this rather lengthy combination of words in the longer title? That is a fair question, and I would offer a straightforward answer. I seek to

address the agency and operations of the Holy Spirit with reference to the act of preaching itself.

I am not addressing the necessity and reality of the agency and operations of the Holy Spirit in our preparations for preaching. There are many ways in which we desperately need His agency and operations prior to our entering into the pulpit. For example, we must experience His work in our preparation as the spirit of wisdom and understanding in the selection of our sermonic materials (Isa. 11:2). We desperately need His guidance when we ask ourselves the question, "What shall I preach?" Further, as we sit at our desks in our studies, we must experience the Spirit's ministry as the spirit of illumination, enabling us to enter into the mind of God in any given text or theme of Scripture. When we pray at the beginning of the preparation of our sermons, "Open thou mine eyes, that I may behold wondrous things out of thy law" (Ps. 119:18), it is the Holy Spirit who brings God's answer to our minds and hearts. Further, we must experience the ministry of the Holy Spirit in our preparation as "the spirit of grace and of supplications" (Zech. 12:10), sustaining in us a prayerful disposition from the beginning to the end of our preparation. These ministries of the Spirit are most necessary and real in the experience of faithful preachers. But I bypass these aspects of His work in order to direct our attention more narrowly to the agency and operations of the Holy Spirit in and on the preacher himself in the very act of preaching.

Again, I am not addressing the agency and operations of the Holy Spirit on the congregation in the act of preaching. Surely, we deeply desire that under our preaching, as it was under the preaching of Peter, the Holy Spirit would fall on all those who hear the Word (Acts 10:44). Rather, I will seek to demonstrate that His agency (His active power) and His operations (the effects of that power) are direct and immediate in and on the preacher in the act of preaching, in contrast to those operations that come through intervening agencies. This, then, is our topical bull's-eye. I trust that the terminology has helped to delimit the field of our concern with some measure of precision.

Important Presuppositions

Second, in this introduction I want briefly to highlight several presuppositions concerning the person and work of the Holy Spirit in general. These presuppositions are realities drawn from a scripturally based and historically orthodox doctrine of the Holy Spirit. I will not take the time to prove these things. I will only attempt to highlight them so that they may function as a kind of present quality control while we meditate and grapple with this often neglected but crucially important dimension of His ministry.

First, I presuppose that the Holy Spirit is a person. When dealing with any aspect of the ministry of the Holy Spirit, whether His gifts or functions, we must always remember these are the operations, gifts, and functions of a person. This truth is particularly vital when considering preaching. An alarm goes off within me when I see expressions like "how to obtain the power of the Spirit in our ministries" or other references to what is called "Holy Spirit power." Such language takes us perilously close to the words of Simon the sorcerer who said to Peter, "Give me also this power." To such crass impersonalizing of the Holy Spirit and the idea that such power could be purchased, Peter responded, "Thy money perish with thee" (Acts 8:19–20). Our present concern is with the agency and operations of one person in relationship to another person, that second person being a preacher.

Second, I also presuppose that He is a divine person. He is God in the fullest sense. All that constitutes the essence of the Father's deity and the Son's deity can and must be equally attributed to the person of the Holy Spirit. Hence, all the reverence, all the submission, and all the love that flows out of Spirit-renewed hearts to the Father and to the Son must also constantly flow out to this glorious divine person called the Holy Spirit.

My third presupposition is that He is also a sovereign, divine person. This fact is especially necessary when thinking of the agency and operations of the Spirit in conjunction with gifts of utterance. The sovereignty of the Holy Spirit is nowhere more highlighted in Scripture than in the very setting of the Apostle Paul's treatment of spiritual gifts in 1 Corinthians 12, where he says, "Now concerning spiritual gifts, brethren, I would not have you ignorant" (v. 1). We are told in verse 11, "But all these worketh that one and the selfsame Spirit, dividing to every man severally [individually] as he will." Therefore we must beware of any attempt to establish ironclad rules within which the Holy Spirit must be expected to operate and function. He does not work in and on the preacher in the act of preaching in any perfectly predictable pattern.

Having explained my lengthier title and identified these three fundamental presuppositions, we now take up our subject under three major headings: 1) its indispensable necessity, 2) its specific manifestations, and 3) its restrained or diminished measure.

CHAPTER 2

❧

The Indispensable Necessity
of the Spirit in Preaching

The Scriptures certainly justify our characterization of this aspect of the ministry of the Spirit as an indispensable necessity. Three categories of biblical witness should persuade you. This dimension of the Spirit's work is not merely a desirable option, and it certainly is not the right of a fanatical fringe of preachers to seek and to claim that they experience such operations of the Holy Spirit. Rather, His agency and operations in the act of preaching are an indispensable necessity for every preacher of the Word of God if his ministry would meet the biblical standard of what preaching ought to be. Three witnesses now arise and testify to the validity of this assertion.

Christ's Ministry
First, it is clear from the Scriptures that such an immediate agency and operation of the Holy Spirit was indispensable to the preaching ministry of our

blessed Lord Jesus Christ Himself. According to the Scriptures, our Lord was conceived by such a work of the Holy Spirit. The angel said to Mary, "The Holy Ghost shall come upon thee, and the power of the Highest shall overshadow thee" (Luke 1:35). The same Holy Spirit who effected the conception of Jesus in the womb of the virgin is the One who nurtured Jesus' holy humanity while He "increased in wisdom and stature, and in favour with God and man" (Luke 2:52). If you are unfamiliar with John Owen's masterful treatise on the person and the work of the Holy Spirit, I urge you to read the section demonstrating His strategic ministry in the development and maturation of the perfect humanity of our Lord Jesus Christ.[1] There was a constant and immediate agency and operation of the Holy Spirit in the human development of our Lord.

Yet, when the time came for Jesus to begin His public ministry, what was the defining work of God with respect to His beloved Son? The answer is very clear from Old Testament prophecy concerning the Messiah. Isaiah proclaimed that the Messiah would be able to say, "The Spirit of the Lord GOD is upon me; because the LORD hath anointed me to preach (Isa. 61:1). We have the historical fulfillment of that prophetic utterance recorded in the gospel of Luke.

---

1. *A Discourse on the Holy Spirit*, in *The Works of John Owen* (Edinburgh: Banner of Truth Trust, 1996), 3: 159–88.

"Now when all the people were baptized, it came to pass, that Jesus also being baptized, and praying, the heaven was opened, and the Holy Ghost descended in a bodily shape like a dove upon him, and a voice came from heaven, which said, Thou art my beloved Son; in thee I am well pleased" (Luke 3:21–22).

Then Jesus was driven into the wilderness by the Spirit who had come upon Him, there to be tempted for forty days and nights by the devil (Luke 4:1–2). He came out of that temptation victorious. Further, "Jesus returned in the power of the Spirit into Galilee: and there went out a fame of him through all the region round about" (Luke 4:14). Think of it. His was incarnate wisdom; pure, unsullied, untainted humanity; gifts of insight and gifts of expression of such a nature and measure that at age twelve He astounded the doctors of the law. Surely, all He needed was a further unfolding of that process of maturation under the superintending agency and operations of the Holy Spirit—but no! There is no record that He uttered a single word of public ministry until He received a special endowment of the Holy Spirit that, among other things, equipped Him to speak as God's authoritative prophet, as well as setting Him apart and sustaining Him so that He finally, by the same "eternal Spirit offered himself without spot to God" (Heb. 9:14). This, then, is the first line of evidence concerning the necessity of the immediate agency and operations of the Spirit in the act of preaching. If even the Lord Jesus needed the Holy Spirit in this way for preaching ministry, so do we.

The Apostles' Ministry

Second, such an immediate agency and operation of the Spirit was indispensable for the apostles. Jesus gave them special endowments of power in conjunction with their appointment as apostles and sent them forth into their Judean ministry (Matt. 10:1). They could "heal the sick, cleanse the lepers, raise the dead, cast out devils [demons]" (Matt. 10:8). The Lord Jesus continued instructing them during the remainder of His earthly ministry. For forty days subsequent to His death and resurrection, He enlarged their understanding concerning the very heart of His mission (see Acts 1:3; Luke 24:45–48). During this period He cleared the fog from their minds about so many Scriptures that they had never really understood. Then they began to enjoy great insight about the spiritual nature of the kingdom He came to establish and the momentous concerns of their Lord's messianic mission. Even after imparting such great spiritual advantages and enlargement of their understanding, Jesus still told them of their need to wait for the promise of the Father, that is, the Holy Spirit, by whom they would be clothed "with power from on high" (Luke 24:49).

Admittedly, these verses record transitional activities in the unrepeatable unfolding of redemptive history. These activities are rightly designated as "programmatic," recording what God was doing in the execution of His redemptive plan, but not "paradigmatic," a pattern of God's activity to be expected throughout subsequent church history. Nevertheless, notice this in particular: in contrast with the broader aspects of the ministry of the Spirit laid out so wonderfully in the Upper Room Discourse of our Lord (John 13–16), here in Luke 24:49, and again in Acts 1:8, Jesus emphasizes the Spirit's ministry in conjunction with power—power directly related to the apostles' bearing witness to the central truths of the gospel. That is precisely the emphasis present when Jesus said in Acts 1:7–8, "It is not for you to know the times or the seasons, which the Father hath put in his own power. But ye shall receive power, after that the Holy Ghost is come upon you: and ye shall be witnesses unto me."

Our Lord highlights power for witness-bearing in His promise of the Pentecostal blessing. Then, when Luke records the actual coming of the Spirit, where does he place the emphasis? Acts 2 informs us unambiguously, "And when the day of Pentecost was fully come, they were all with one accord in one place. And suddenly there came a sound from heaven as of a rushing mighty wind, and it filled all the house where they were sitting. And there appeared unto them cloven tongues like as of fire, and it sat upon each of them. And they were all filled with the Holy Ghost, and began to speak with other tongues, as the Spirit gave them utterance" (Acts 2:1–4).

The text does not say that "they were all filled with the Holy Spirit and had an immediate sense of the wonder of their union with Christ." According to the Upper Room Discourse, such a consciousness would have been one of the immediate operations of the Spirit along with many other promised blessings. But notice what is highlighted by the Spirit of God through Luke's pen: the text says that "they were all filled with the Holy Ghost, and began to speak …as the Spirit gave them utterance." This is the fundamental paradigm for new covenant ministry. Filled with the Spirit, they spoke as the Spirit gave them utterance. Here was a work of the Spirit that was immediate in connection with their speaking "the wonderful works of God" (Acts 2:11). Admittedly, there was a supernatural and programmatic dimension to these events having special significance in redemptive history. They were given the ability to speak in dialects and languages that they had not acquired in the ordinary way. This element was indeed programmatic, not paradigmatic. It is beyond our present scope of concern to demonstrate this fact from Scripture.

However, the strong emphasis we can see unfolding throughout the book of Acts is that the Spirit is present in His agency and operations in conjunction with utterance that, again and again, is described as bold utterance. It was proclamation prompted and made possible only by the present agency and operation of the Spirit. This was a conscious experience of the apostolic band. It was not something they took by faith and simply believed it was happening outside the realm of their spiritual consciousness. No, both Paul and the Thessalonians knew that the Spirit's special agency and operations were present in Paul's preaching to them. In his first letter to the Thessalonians he was able to affirm without any fear of contradiction that "our gospel came not unto you in word only, but also in power, and in the Holy Ghost, and in much assurance; as ye know what manner of men we were among you for your sake" (1 Thess. 1:5).

Again, he wrote similarly to the Corinthians: "And I, brethren, when I came to you…I was with you in weakness, and in fear, and in much trembling"; that is, this was his conscious, personal, internal, dispositional experience. "And my speech and my preaching was not with enticing words of man's wisdom"; that is, this was his conscious speaking experience with reference to the content and rhetorical style of his preaching. "But in demonstration of the Spirit and of power"; that is, this was his conscious speaking experience with reference to the agency and operations of the Holy Spirit in the very act of his preaching (from 1 Cor. 2:1–4). When Peter describes the preaching of the apostles, he uses these words: "them that have preached the gospel unto you with the Holy Ghost sent down from heaven" (1 Peter 1:12).

Hence, I affirm that the necessity of the Holy Spirit's agency and operation in the act of preaching is seen with reference to our blessed Lord and in the preaching experience of the apostles.

New Covenant Ministry

Third, such an immediate agency and operation of the Spirit is an indispensable component of any God-appointed ministry of the new covenant. I commend to you a careful evaluation and study of 2 Corinthians 2:14–4:18. In this passage we are given the apostle's teaching on the nature of the new covenant ministry as having greater glory than the ministry of the old covenant. In the heart of this section, chapter 3:1–8, there is a dominant emphasis on the ministry of the Spirit. So much is this the case that the term "ministry of the Spirit" is synonymous with the new covenant. Paul clearly states this fact: "Not that we are sufficient of ourselves to think any thing as of ourselves; but our sufficiency is of God; who also hath made us able ministers of the new testament [i.e., the new covenant]; not of the letter, but of the spirit" (2 Cor. 3:5–6). In Paul's mind, to be made a minister of the new covenant is to be constituted a minister of the Spirit.

I have laid before the reader in a brief way the threefold testimony concerning what I have called the indispensable necessity for the immediate agency and operation of the Holy Spirit on us as preach-ers in the act of preaching. Just as this immediate agency and operation is described and promised in conjunction with the activity of prayer in Romans 8:26, so it is available to us in the act of preaching through the virtue of Christ's own commitment to His servants and in virtue of our union with Him. Just as we do not know how to pray as we ought but the Spirit helps us in that dilemma by His personal agency and operation, so He helps us in the situation of our helplessness to preach as we ought.

At this point, I give you the first of several quotes from Charles H. Spurgeon's marvelous chapter in his book, *Lectures to My Students*. The chapter is entitled "The Holy Spirit in Conjunction with Our Minis-tries." Listen to what Spurgeon says concerning the indispensability of the Spirit's agency and operations in connection with our preaching ministry.

> To us, as ministers, the Holy Spirit is absolutely essential. Without him our office is a mere name. We claim no priesthood over and above

that which belongs to every child of God; but we are the successors of those who, in olden times, were moved of God to declare his word, to testify against transgression, and to plead his cause. Unless we have the spirit of the prophets resting upon us, the mantle which we wear is nothing but a rough garment to deceive. We ought to be driven forth with abhorrence from the society of honest men for daring to speak in the name of the Lord if the Spirit of God rests not upon us. We believe ourselves to be spokesmen for Jesus Christ, appointed to continue his witness upon earth; but upon him and his testimony the Spirit of God always rested, and if it does not rest upon us, we are evidently not sent forth into the world as he was. At Pentecost the commencement of the great work of converting the world was with flaming tongues and a rushing mighty wind, symbols of the presence of the Spirit; if, therefore, we think to succeed without the Spirit, we are not after the Pentecostal order. If we have not the Spirit which Jesus promised, we cannot perform the commission which Jesus gave.[2]

---

2. Charles H. Spurgeon, *Lectures to My Students* (Edinburgh: Banner of Truth, 2008), 225.

CHAPTER 3

❧

Specific Manifestations of the Spirit in Preaching

Let us consider some of the specific manifestations of the Spirit's immediate agency and operation on the preacher in the act of preaching. I am not attempting to be comprehensive or exhaustive. I would merely highlight four of these specific manifestations.

A Heightened Sense

First, if and when the Holy Spirit is resting upon us as we preach, He will often give us what I have chosen to call a heightened sense of the spiritual realities in which we are trafficking as we preach. Let me describe the process. Prior to coming into the pulpit you sit at your desk in a prayerful frame. You believe you have been guided by several strands of influence, both within and without, to settle on the text or subject you purpose to preach. You may be preaching through an entire book of Scripture. You may be preaching a series on a given theme of Scripture. At your desk you engage all of your faculties in the labor of accurate exegesis, clear organization, vivid illustration, pointed application, and all of the disciplines that go into responsible sermon preparation. You ponder the truth as you seek to come to a more accurate grasp of it and how best to lay it out before your people on the Lord's Day. As you do these things, you experience a felt impression of the truth on your own spirit. It may be truth that causes your spirit to groan with spiritual pain. It may be truth that causes you to back off from your desk and raise your hands and give vent to a spontaneous "Hallelujah!" It may be a truth that causes you to shed tears. In other words, in the process of your preparation, you experience genuine emotional as well as intellectual engagement with the truth you are preparing to preach.

Finally the time set apart for sermon preparation has come to an end. The moment of truth has arrived. We place our notes or manuscript in a folder and leave the study in order to seek a decent night of rest before the labors of the Lord's Day. I know at this point most of us pastors would love to have an eight-day week. We think to ourselves, "If only I had one more Saturday, how much better I would preach!" If any preacher has never felt that reality, I would like to know his secret.

The Lord's Day comes and you stand before the

people of God in a prayerful frame, having met with God in the early hours of the morning. You begin to convey to the congregation the fruit of your labors in the study. As you begin to preach, your mind begins to experience the warmth that comes from the friction of the truth on your own spirit. In living interaction with the people of God to whom you are preaching and in the promised special presence of God among His gathered people, you are conscious of a spiritual current that has been established between you and your congregation. Now, the truth that flooded your soul in the study with 100 watts of a divine influence of spiritual light and 100 BTUs of spiritual heat—that very truth, not another (and certainly not an extemporaneously conceived error)—is now augmented to 1000 watts of light in your mind and 1000 BTUs of heat in your own spirit. It stands out in bold three-dimensional relief in the act of preaching. The truth that exerted its emotional energy on you with heaviness, joy, grief, and other pressures on your spirit in the study is now greatly intensifying its pressure on the entirety of your inner life. Perhaps you meditated on some aspect of the glory of Christ in the study, coming to your pulpit feeling so incompetent to set forth that glory. Your tongue seemed thick, your mind sluggish, and your heart a mass of dullness. But then, in the act of preaching, by the immediate agency and operation of the Holy Spirit, you are enabled to get a sight of the glory of Christ to such a degree that there is a sense in which you would not care if everyone got up and walked out of the building! Your preaching about the glory of Christ has become almost a sacred soliloquy about your Savior—an internal rapture in the act of preaching. On the other hand, you may have been reflecting on the horrors of hell in your studies and pulpit preparations. There was a heaviness of heart as you did so. You said to yourself, "How can I preach on this horrific doctrine with such a dull heart?" But in the act of preaching it is as though you are given the ability to smell the brimstone and to hear the hopeless cry of the damned, and your soul feels the horrors of the pit that awaits the impenitent. You preach the truth of hell as one who senses and feels the reality of what you are preaching. What are these experiences? They are nothing other and nothing less than the blessed reality of the immediate agency and operation of the Holy Spirit in our preaching, giving us a heightened sense of the spiritual realities in which we are trafficking as we preach.

One of the results of this blessed experience is that at times it will give an involuntary glow to the very countenance of the preacher. No actor can produce it. There is nothing in your notes that says "glow here." You cannot anticipate it; you cannot force or imitate it. It may evoke an unplanned and unforced tear in the eye. At other times it will inject an element of pathos and pleading power into the vocal cords and in many ways take a preacher totally out of himself. My dear reader, if you are a preacher and do not find these things resonating with you in terms of things you have experienced, both you and your hearers are to be pitied. This is why George Whitefield said, "I would not for one thousand worlds preach an unfelt Christ." This is what White-field was talking about.

Again, I quote Spurgeon. He writes the following words in that same chapter concerning the work of the Holy Spirit in connection with our ministry:

> The divine Spirit will sometimes work upon us so as to bear us completely out of ourselves. From the beginning of the sermon to the end we might of such times say, "Whether in the body or out of it I cannot tell: God knoweth." Everything has been forgotten but the one all-engrossing subject in hand.
>
> If I were forbidden to enter heaven, but were permitted to select my state for all eternity, I should choose to be as I sometimes feel in preaching the gospel. Heaven is foreshadowed in such a state: the mind shut out from all disturbing influences, adoring the majestic and consciously present God, every faculty aroused and joyously excited to its utmost capability,

all the thoughts and powers of the soul joy-
ously occupied in contemplating the glory of
the Lord, and extolling to listening crowds
the Beloved of our soul; and all the while the
purest conceivable benevolence towards one's
fellow creatures urging the heart to plead with
them on God's behalf—what state of mind
can rival this? Alas, we have reached this
ideal, but we cannot always maintain it, for
we know also what it is to preach in chains,
or beat the air. We may not attribute holy and
happy changes in our ministry to anything less
than the action of the Holy Spirit upon our
souls. I am sure the Spirit does so work.[1]

Dare we write off these words of Spurgeon as the
undisciplined utterances of a fanatical mystic? Dare
we dismiss all this by attributing his sentiments to
an overly emotional temperament? To ask such questions is to answer them. No, they are the words of
a sane and articulate Calvinist who knew what it
was to experience the immediate agency and operations of the Holy Spirit in the act of preaching—an
agency and operation that produced in him a heightened sense of the spiritual realities in which he was
trafficking as he preached.

---

1. Charles H. Spurgeon, *Lectures to My Students* (Edinburgh: Banner of Truth, 2008), 231.

Unfettered Liberty

But not only does the immediate agency and operation of the Spirit give us the above described experience when we preach, but second, the Holy Spirit gives us in the act of preaching the blessed experience of an unfettered liberty and a heightened facility of utterance. I said earlier that the paradigm for preaching in the new covenant is Acts 2:4—filled with the Spirit, they spoke "as the Spirit gave them utterance." I am especially thankful for chapter 4 in the book of Acts, where tongues are no longer in the picture. Notice how the same paradigm remains. The preaching servants of God responded to open opposition by gathering to pray. As they prayed, the Spirit of God came upon them in a fresh and powerful way. We read in Acts 4:31, "And when they had prayed, the place was shaken where they were assembled together; and they were all filled with the Holy Ghost, and they spake the word of God with boldness." The word translated "boldness," a noun sometimes used in verbal form, is the dominant word used to describe the quality of the preaching recorded throughout the book of Acts. Simply take your concordance and trace out the use of that family of words.

This emphasis on "preaching with boldness" culminates in the apostle Paul's request of the Ephesian believers that they would pray for him (see Eph. 6:19–20). And what was the prayer request he left with those believers? He asked them to pray on his behalf "that utterance may be given unto me, that I may open my mouth boldly, to make known the mystery of the gospel, for which I am an ambassador in bonds: that therein I may speak boldly, as I ought to speak." Note that the apostle asks them to pray that boldness would be given to him. He knows the mystery of the gospel. He does not ask them to pray that God will unfold that mystery to him. However, he is deeply concerned that he will be enabled to speak that mystery as he ought to speak it. This "boldness" in one sense has nothing to do with natural temperament or with native loquaciousness. It has nothing to do with past enablings. It has everything to do with an immediate agency and operation of the Holy Spirit on the preacher that he might experience unfettered liberty and a heightened facility of utterance.

When the mind of the preacher sees truth with that intensified light of the Spirit's assistance in the act of preaching, and his heart is expanded with greater measures of what the old writers would call "disinterested benevolence" (a genuine and selfless love for others), what greater frustration could there be than to see truth with heightened clarity, and to feel an intense yearning that others profit from that truth, only to have it all dammed up in the mind, the vocal cords, and on the tongue? Alas,

I know something of that frustration. However, the Spirit delights to come to us in the act of preaching with the blessed experience of unfettered liberty and a heightened facility of utterance, so that there are times when we are tempted to ask the congregation to excuse us while we write down the very things that have come out of our mouths! With all of our arduous labors in the study, we simply could not state the truth the way we have just stated it in the pulpit. The Holy Spirit at times even gives us an ability to draw words out of the storeroom of our vocabularies—words we may not have used for many months or years—yet suddenly they flash into our consciousness when we are preaching. We reflect later and say to ourselves, "That very thing that came to me in the act of preaching is the thing I was fishing for in the study, but could not retrieve." At such points in our preaching, our hearts are lifted up in praise and thanksgiving to God. There are times when we would like to pause in the midst of our preaching and ask the congregation for permission to get on our faces to worship and say, "Oh God, thank you, thank you."

Admittedly, there are times when this experience leaves us vulnerable to the wretched sin of pride. However, more often we are humbled, deeply humbled. We know that what came out of our mouths was completely due to a present and pow-

erful operation of the Spirit of God on the entirety
of our redeemed humanity. At such times we know
it would be as irrational to think that we created
ourselves as to think that we, unaided by the Holy
Spirit, produced what has just come out of our
mouths. It was this person, God the Holy Spirit,
operating in and on our persons in conjunction with
the proclamation of His glorious truth. Marvelous,
wonderful, blessed experience!

In making the above claims of "unfettered liberty and a heightened facility of utterance," we do not
claim an experience that rises to the utterly unique
operations of the Spirit given to the prophets or to the
penmen of the Holy Scriptures when they were made
the instruments of conveying divine revelation. I do
wish, however, to commend the real and felt experience I am describing as a biblical avenue for churches
enjoying what they might refer to as a "prophetic
word." The practice of speaking supposed words from
the Lord in the divine first person (e.g., "My people,
I am about to pour out My favor upon you!") is often
a sincere but misguided blurring of the fundamental
truth of the finality of Scripture. The less dangerous
"prophetic word" that often comes in the category of
edifying speech (Eph. 4:29) is an anemic substitute
for the kind of unction and freedom in preaching
that churches need. The people of God desperately
need and should expect fresh, potent words from the

Lord, and such will be found in the careful exposition and penetrating application of biblical texts under the influence of the immediate agency of the Spirit's power on godly and gifted preachers.

There were incidents that I remember from the days when we had the Trinity Ministerial Academy functioning as a ministry of Trinity Baptist Church. The academy was a four-year, seminary-level school for training men for the ministry. Now I do not want to romanticize these things and touch up the facts. That would be easy to do with the passing of time, but the following kind of incident happened more than once. One of the young men would go off to preach on the weekend. If he were a novice at preaching, I would try to get to him sometime shortly after his preaching experience and ask him, "Brother, how did things go for you?" Then I would listen carefully to the young man. More than once he would describe something like this: "Well, pastor, I prepared such and such a sermon and I was about a third of the way into the sermon when something strange happened." He would then begin to try to describe what happened when the Spirit of God came upon him by His special immediate agency and operation, giving him a heightened ability of utterance. I would play dumb and act as though I were listening to someone tinged with a bit of fanaticism. I would say, in effect, "My brother, what are you talking about? Tell me some more." He was trying to describe what is in reality indescribable. However, from that point onward he could never doubt that there was such a reality as the presence and power of the Spirit in the preaching of the Word. I would then say to the young man, "My brother, you have tasted this reality and you will never be satisfied with anything less again." Some call it unction, some call it liberty, and some will say they were "especially helped in preaching." Whatever we call it, this reality must never be treated as something that is in the realm of fanaticism. Having tasted it, a preacher cannot be satisfied without it. Again, I hide behind C. H. Spurgeon. In the same chapter we have been quoting, he went on to say:

> Brethren, we require the Holy Spirit also to incite us in our utterance. I doubt not you are all conscious of different states of mind in preaching. Some of those states arise from your body being in different conditions. A bad cold will not only spoil the clearness of the voice, but freeze the flow of the thoughts. For my own part if I cannot speak clearly I am unable to think clearly, and the matter becomes hoarse as well as the voice. The stomach, also, and all the other organs of the body, affect the mind; but it is not to these things that I allude. Are you not conscious of changes altogether independent of the body? When

you are in robust health do you not find your-
selves one day as heavy as Pharaoh's chariots
with the wheels taken off, and at another time
as much at liberty as "a hind let loose"? Today
your branch glitters with the dew, yesterday it
was parched with drought. Who knoweth not
that the Spirit of God is in all this? [2]

These are not the words of a fanatical and fly-
by-night preacher. They are the words of a sane,
balanced, humble, and greatly used servant of God
whose usefulness continues around the world in
amazing ways even to this hour.

An Enlarged Heart

Not only does this immediate agency and operation of the Holy Spirit in our preaching give us a
heightened and felt sense of the realities in which we
traffic, a blessed experience of liberty of utterance,
and a heightened facility of speech, but in the third
place, the Holy Spirit gives us in the act of preaching
an enlarged heart, presently suffused with increased
measures of selfless love that yearns to do our hearers good by means of our preaching. In taking up
this strand of our study, I remind you of the sobering truth of 1 Corinthians 13:1–3. There we are told
that "though I speak with the tongues of men and of

2. Spurgeon, *Lectures to My Students*, 231.

angels, and have not charity [love],…I am nothing…
[and] it profiteth me nothing."

While we are at our desks the dominant disposition of our hearts is often, and rightly so, one of
seeking to labor in the study with 2 Timothy 2:15
ever before us as a standard for our labors. Paul uses
an imperative of the verb *spoudazo*. In that text, Paul
says to Timothy and to us, "Marshal and engage
all of your faculties to show yourself approved unto
God, a workman who has no just cause for shame
before his Master as you handle the word of truth
with accuracy and integrity." Sitting at our desks, we
are conscious that the eyes of our Master are on us
as we are preparing to handle His Word of truth.
When we have so labored as to believe that we can
present to our Master what we are prepared to say in
His name, then the disposition that dominates to a
greater degree (though one cannot put these things
into isolated categories) is how this will do good to
our people. You bring your congregation into the
study with you. You see their faces and think of
their states and conditions, especially when it comes
to the area of application and illustration. You say
within yourself, "Lord, how can I make this truth
plainer to the children, and how can I make it reso-
nate more with the man behind his workbench and
the stressed young mother seeking to care for her
little ones and her husband? Lord, how can I con-

struct arrows fashioned out of this truth to pierce the hearts of the careless and the wandering? How can I bring a word of comfort to the grieving and the distressed?" These mental exercises are aspects of divine love for your people, love that is willing to enter into the sacrificial labor of thoughtful and careful exposition, application, and illustration. These prayers reveal that there are measures of divine love for your people operative in your heart while you are at the desk in your sermon preparation.

However, you now stand to preach, and you are looking into those very same faces. They are no longer an image imported by an activity of the mind into the study, but real flesh-and-blood people sitting in front of you. The Spirit of God, whose fruit is love, expands your heart and fills it with new dimensions of yearning love for your people. Your love for them at this point indeed fills you with a passion to do them good. It is then that you almost instinctively find yourself echoing the words of the apostle when he said, "O ye Corinthians, our mouth is open unto you, our heart is enlarged" (2 Cor. 6:11).

The conjunction of an open heart and an open mouth is forged by an enlarged measure of love, and it is that enlarged heart infused with fresh measures of love that is the mother of genuine earnestness and unfeigned passion. The worst counsel to give any preacher is to tell him that he needs to put more earnestness into his preaching. No, we must feel more deeply the impulses of divine love that, in turn, will produce genuine earnestness and passion. Someone has defined earnestness as follows: "It is the energy of the soul intent on a given object." I like that. Think of a young man sitting before you who is intent on a given object. That object is one of the young ladies in your church. If he were not in earnest, he would have been scared away already because the young lady upon whom he has set his eyes has a godly and protective father, a man who is persuaded from the Scriptures that a father has a solemn responsibility to be involved in the romantic interests of his daughter. However, the interested young man has an intention in his soul, and that intention produces some real earnestness. He is willing to sit down face to face with that father and not be spooked away from the pursuit of the young lady. He expresses the energy of his soul, which is now intent on gaining the object of his interest.

Well, brethren, what are we doing in the pulpit? Are we merely earning a living, trafficking in noble and religious notions? Do we really desire to see sinners saved? Do we genuinely long to see the people of God brought to greater maturity in Christ? Do we believe that the things we convey in our preaching will, with the blessing of God, produce those very things for which we yearn? If the answer to these

questions is yes, then how can we help but be pas-
sionate and earnest? Remember the words of the late
Professor John Murray: "To me, preaching without
passion is not preaching at all."[3] Here are the words
of J. W. Alexander in his profoundly helpful book,
Thoughts on Preaching: "The same truths uttered from
the pulpit by different men, or by the same man in
different states of feeling, will produce very different
effects. Some of these are far beyond what the bare
conviction of the truth so uttered would ordinarily
produce. The whole mass of truth, by the sudden
passion of the speaker, is made red-hot and burns its
way. Passion is eloquence."[4]

These are not the words of a convinced Armin-
ian. They are from a man who had no sympathy for
the emotional manipulation of his hearers. They
come from a proven, scholarly, experiential Calvinist known for his extraordinary competence as
a preacher. It is a grievous thing to hear otherwise
orthodox and Reformed preachers say, in effect, with
regard to their own preaching, "What I am giving
is God's truth, and if He has determined to bless
it, He will bless it, regardless of my felt and conscious experience of any present yearning born of

---

3. *The Collected Writings of John Murray* (Edinburgh: Banner
of Truth, 1982), 3:72.

4. J. W. Alexander, *Thoughts on Preaching* (Edinburgh: Banner of Truth, 1975), 20.

love for the well-being of my hearers." While there is a sliver of truth in such an attitude, that sliver has been stretched into a massive canopy under which preaching without the present and powerful agency and operation of the Holy Spirit is tolerated and excused. The reason God has ordained preaching as His unique method for dismantling the kingdom of darkness and building the kingdom of His Son has more to it than the bare statement of truth. God has given this unique place to preaching because in preaching, the effect of truth on the redeemed man who preaches is both manifested and embodied in the very act of conveying that truth. Alexander recognized this when he wrote that "the whole mass of truth, by the sudden passion of the speaker, is made red-hot and burns its way." Ask yourself: When has God ordinarily burned His truth into your heart under preaching so as to elicit a righteous response? Was it under an orthodox but "take it or leave it" preacher? No, I believe you will say that truth worked its way into your heart when truth, as it were, gathered to itself the energy of the love-suffused soul of the preacher and came throbbing with the energy of that love to your ear and registered in your mind and heart by the blessing of the Holy Spirit. No little part of that spiritual experience is to be found in the fact that you sensed and could not deny that the preacher was conveying to you dimensions of divine love that yearned to do you good by his preaching. This was the present ministry of the Holy Spirit in the heart of the preacher. I believe that few men would live long if God were continually to sustain in their hearts the measure of selfless love experienced during the act of preaching. Could it be that the early death of Brainerd and the untimely death of M'Cheyne affirm this statement?

Heightened Confidence in the Word

The fourth manifestation of the Holy Spirit's immediate agency and operation on the preacher in the act of preaching is a heightened sense of the absolute authority, sufficiency, and trustworthiness of the Scriptures. This fact gives a compelling authority to the ministry of any man who preaches "not with enticing words of man's wisdom, but in demonstration of the Spirit and of power" (1 Cor. 2:4).

The teaching of Calvin, and its later embodiment in the Westminster Confession of Faith and in those confessions of faith that took the majority of their substance from it, are all agreed in their answer to the basic question, "How can we be persuaded that our Bibles are the very Word of God?" After referring to the various things that may incline us to accept the Scriptures as the Word of God, the confession states: "Yet notwithstanding, our full persuasion, and assurance of the infallible truth, and divine authority thereof, is from the inward work of the Holy Spirit, bearing witness by and with the Word in our hearts."[5]

What is true of the ordinary believer respecting his confidence that his Bible is the Word of God comes in a heightened way to the preacher in the act of preaching by the ministry of the Holy Spirit. If you are a preacher, surely you have felt as I have many times while preaching the Word of God that you stood forty feet tall with a sword ten feet long and six inches wide. You felt that you could take on anyone and anything with that "sword of the Spirit." Now this sense of the absolute authority of the Word of God is not a qualitatively different conviction concerning the Scriptures — a difference in kind from that with which you entered the pulpit. Rather, it is a heightened persuasion that, in turn, gives a note of unanswerable authority to your preaching. Since our preaching deals with God's revealed truth, should we not expect the "Spirit of truth" to be unusually active and present as we preach, attesting to our own hearts with power that His Word is indeed truth?

It was this element of authority that marked the ministry of our Lord Jesus and constantly astonished His hearers. This fact is repeatedly emphasized in the Gospels. In very differing contexts, the Gospel writers highlight the astonishment men had in the

---

5. The 1689 London Baptist Confession of Faith, I.5.

face of the authority of our Lord's preaching and teaching. Whether He was preaching and teaching in the open air or in the synagogue, authority marked His ministry (see Matt. 7:28–29; Mark 1:22; Luke 4:31–32). We must constantly underscore to our people that we are neither prophets nor infallible interpreters of the Word of God. Yet we do not come before them merely to "share" or to "suggest" or to "join them in their quest for truth." Rather, we come before them as heralds of the living God to announce the message of our King. As we do so, and as the Holy Spirit rests on us in power, we will experience in our own hearts this blessed and wonderful sense of a heightened conviction that we are indeed bringing the message of our King.

These, then, are four specific manifestations of the agency and operations of the Holy Spirit in and on the preacher in the act of preaching. I ask the reader: Which of them would you deem to be dispensable or optional? Which of them would you regard as a luxury and not absolutely essential to a God-glorifying and consistently edifying ministry of the Word? I trust that the description of these four manifestations has found an echo in the experience of every preacher and of every child of God who reads these pages.

CHAPTER 4

❧

Restrained or Diminished Measure of the Spirit in Preaching

If you have been persuaded that the manifestations of the Spirit's work in preaching is absolutely essential to a ministry of the new covenant, then you will be prepared to give serious consideration to the things that tend to diminish it. Therefore, we must turn our attention to the issues related to the restraining or the withdrawing of the Spirit's powerful agency and operations in our ministry.

Explaining "Restrained" and "Diminished"

First, I will define what I mean by the words "restrained" and "diminished" and then give a necessary word of qualification. When something is restrained, it is held back. It never moves fully in the direction that it desires or intends to go. For example, when the floodwaters of a swollen river threaten to inundate the countryside, they are restrained by the influence of a levee. I am using that word to express

the conviction that there are men who have known
little if any of the immediate agency and operation
of the Holy Spirit in their preaching because in their
experience, the Spirit has been restrained. They
have never come to their full inheritance in Christ
in terms of the presence and operation of the Holy
Spirit in and on them in the act of preaching. In that
sense, His ministry is restrained in them.

On the other hand, there are some in whom His
agency and operation are diminished. That is, they
have known measures of His influence in the past
that they now no longer experience. Like Samson,
they have gone forth into spiritual warfare and "wist
not that the LORD was departed from" them (Judg.
16:20). This is the sense in which I am using the
words "restrained" and "diminished."

I would make a necessary qualification. Some
aspects of the restraining and diminishing of the
Spirit's immediate agency and operation on a
preacher in the act of preaching can only be resolved
in recognizing the reality of the inscrutable and
absolute sovereignty of God. We learn from church
history and Christian biography that there are men
who had periods in their life and ministry when
there was a universally acknowledged, copious measure of the Spirit's power resting on their preaching.
However, it was for a recognizable period of time.
We know from their testimony and their subsequent

history, validated by intimate friends, that there was no evident spiritual, moral, or doctrinal deviation that would have grieved or quenched the Spirit. Rather, their experience was due to the sovereign, unexplained, and free operation of the Holy Spirit in which God demonstrated that He retains His right to be God. This truth must be kept constantly before us whenever we come to a subject such as seeking to ascertain the reasons for a restrained or diminished measure of the Spirit's immediate agency and operations on men in the act of preaching. However, with that qualification conditioning how we think, I am bold to assert that there are yet general and discernible patterns and principles that we must acknowledge and with which we must honestly reckon when we ask the question, "Why have I not attained a greater measure of the Spirit's immediate agency and operations in my preaching?" or, "Why do I experience less of that agency now than I have known in the past?" I will now address some basic reasons for this reality.

Disregarding the Necessity of the Spirit

The first is that the immediate agency and operations of the Spirit may be restrained or diminished because the necessity for these realities is not regarded as indispensable by the preacher himself. We know from our Bibles that the Holy Spirit can sovereignly come upon even a dumb animal, such as Balaam's donkey, so that the lips, the tongue, and the vocal apparatus of the donkey speak the very words of the living God to a renegade prophet. Saul can be found meandering among the prophets and the Spirit of God can descend upon him, causing him to prophesy. However, the Holy Spirit, who is a divine person, generally does not provide gracious and copious measures of His agency and operation where His presence and power are not treasured, earnestly sought, believingly expected, and jealously guarded.

For some, this attitude of relative indifference to the experience of the Spirit's agency and operation is the fruit of a false and unbiblical view of preaching that regards the ministry of the Spirit in the study as all that is really necessary for an effective ministry. Anything beyond this is considered a quasi-charismatic notion or something bordering on a kooky fanaticism or an experience limited to certain types of personalities. Others fail to regard this aspect of the Spirit's ministry as essential because of a deeply rooted core of carnal self-confidence, a confidence that puts them under a dimension of God's curse rather than His blessing. A passage that has been a lifetime companion with me in conjunction with preaching is Jeremiah 17:5–9. These verses begin with the sobering words, "Thus saith the LORD; Cursed be the man that trusteth in man, and maketh flesh his arm, and whose heart departeth from the LORD." God goes on to describe such a man in graphic terms as being like a parched, burned out, blasted, and unfruitful field. Such words are a frightening but accurate description of some men's ministry, because they do not have an internal disposition of being utterly weaned from confidence in themselves. There is in them a deep persuasion (although it would be difficult for them to acknowledge it) that the most real and necessary ministry of the Spirit is what is experienced in the study. They wrongly think that fundamentally all the Spirit does in and with the preacher when he is in the pulpit is to help him make sure that he keeps his wits about him and is able to get out from his notes what he believes God has given him in his preparation. There is little or no belief in, earnest prayer for, and expectation of any specific and distinct operation of the Holy Spirit in the preacher in the actual act of preaching. Oh yes, there may be the prayer, "Lord, make the fruit of my study and my work in the secret place fruitful in my people as I enter the pulpit," but there is no expectation that anything fundamentally different will happen in the preacher's own heart, mind, and tongue. There is no expectation of a heightened sense of spiritual realities, an unfettered liberty of utterance, an enlarged heart of love, or a greater sense of the authority of Scripture, all of which, as we have seen, are evidences of the immediate agency and operation of the Holy Spirit in and on the preacher in the act of preaching.

For others, the failure to believe in these dimensions of the Spirit's ministry as a necessary component of true biblical preaching is patent in their lack of specific and focused prayer for such a ministry of the Holy Spirit. For these men James 4:2 is a searching indictment: "ye have not, because ye ask not." In Luke 11:5–13 we have the record of our Lord's teaching concerning the necessity of importunity in our prayers. The climactic statement in that passage focuses on the necessity of importunity in connection with praying for God's good gift of the Holy Spirit to be given to us. In verse 13 our Lord said, "If ye then, being evil, know how to give good gifts unto your children: how much more shall your heavenly Father give the Holy Spirit to them that ask him?" Men in the present category reason within themselves, "Does not God say that the word that goes forth from His mouth shall be blessed and will not return unto Him void? And since I am seeking to speak His Word faithfully, why do I need specifically to pray for the presence and power of the Holy Spirit to rest upon me in that exercise?"

At this point I offer my own testimony. Some years ago I was convicted that I was not taking Luke 11:13 at face value and giving it a more dominant place in my prayers prior to preaching. After confessing my sins of omission, I determined that by the grace of God I would change. I then began to do something that subsequently became a fixed ritual for me.

The distance between my home and the church building could be covered in about twenty minutes. During that time I began to sing to the Lord two choruses that I had learned years ago. In one of them, the words are, "With Thy Spirit fill me, with Thy Spirit fill me. Lord, possess me now I pray, and with Thy Spirit fill me." I then composed a number of individual stanzas to that chorus based on what would happen if God would indeed fill me with His Holy Spirit. Hence, some of the subsequent stanzas went as follows: "With compassion fill me," "With discernment fill me," "With great boldness fill me," "With directness help me," "With fresh unction clothe me," etc. Was there any discernible difference in my preaching subsequent to my engagement in this ritual? I answer by saying that some discerning people who had sat under my ministry for a lengthy period and who had no knowledge of my newly acquired prayer ritual indicated in their own way that they sensed a heightened measure of the enabling of the Spirit of God in my ministry.

I ask you, my preacher brother, do you have a deep-seated conviction that there is such a ministry of the Holy Spirit to be experienced in your preaching? Do you treasure that ministry? Do you earnestly seek it? Do you believingly expect it? Or does God leave you to the mercy of your own pathetic resources as a curse on your subtle form of creature confidence? I leave you to work out the answers to these questions in the searching presence of God.

Grieving the Spirit

A second reason for this restraining or diminishing of the Spirit's operation and agency on the preacher in the act of preaching is that it can be restrained or diminished if the Holy Spirit is being grieved in the life or ministry of the preacher. Here, of course, I am referring to the words of Ephesians 4:30, "And grieve not the holy Spirit of God, whereby ye are sealed unto the day of redemption." Although the theologians and the exegetes have gone all 'round the proverbial mulberry bush talking about the limitations that we must place on anthropopathisms (attributing human capacities and emotions to the Deity), how are we to understand this clear imperative? Well, when God says, "Don't grieve the Holy Spirit," He obviously means that we are not to grieve the Holy Spirit! He is a person who in His personhood reacts to certain situations with a disposition that has kinship with what we experience as the emotion and disposition of grief. With all the due qualifications demanded by the Creator-creature distinction, if God meant to convey that He has no relationship to our felt experience of grief, why did He use this particular word? He did not put it there so that it should be bled of all its significance, thereby projecting the image of a God who is beyond and outside of any feeling akin to our grief. No, He tells us that we are not to grieve the Holy Spirit, for the simple reason that a grieved Spirit becomes an estranged or a withdrawn Spirit.

He does not withdraw as to His indwelling. Those whom He indwells are said to be "sealed unto the day of redemption." But if He is grieved, He generally withdraws His free operation in the same way that your wife, when grieved by your boorishness or insensitivity, withdraws her normal attitude and expression of openness or transparency, her free flow of expressed affection. She does not pull her wedding ring off her finger and throw it out the window, although there may be times when she is tempted to do so. No, she meant the vows that she took when she said, "till death do us part," but an aggrieved wife becomes a withdrawn wife. Therefore, we must not grieve the Holy Spirit. It is the height of spiritual cheekiness to be grieving the Holy Spirit because of an area of ethical controversy with God and then to pray for His special assistance and presence in our preaching. Such praying borders on an attempt to engage in a kind of pagan manipulation of the Deity.

More specifically, how is the Holy Spirit grieved? The immediate context of Ephesians 4:30 shows He is grieved when the people of God commit sins against one another, whether in word, deed, or attitude of heart. However, the larger context, particularly going back to 4:17, suggests that the offense is anything which marks a reversion to the lifestyle of the unconverted pagan. He is the Holy Spirit. Can it be, my brother, that your eyes are now looking with impunity at images on your computer or television screen that at one time would have shocked and horrified you? Is it that now you rationalize that your looking is an outworking of a more mature understanding of the doctrine of Christian liberty? If so, then the absence of the Spirit's power on your pulpit endeavors is an eloquent testimony to the fact that you have grieved Him by this moral compromise. Is not the Spirit grieved when angry and sharp words are spoken to your wife or children, and those words are not scripturally dealt with in the way of both vertical and horizontal repentance and cleansing? If we would have biblical grounds to expect the immediate agency and operation of the Holy Spirit in and on us in our preaching, we must be able to say with the apostle Paul, "I know nothing by [against] myself" (1 Cor. 4:4). Further, we must also be able to say with the apostle, "And herein do I exercise myself, to have always a conscience void of offence toward God, and toward men" (Acts 24:16).

I would suggest also that the Holy Spirit is grieved by more than this. In broader terms, He is also called "the Spirit of truth" (John 14:17). As such, He has come to bear witness to the truth and to give His unction and power to the servant of God who is speaking His truth. Surely then, the Holy Spirit is grieved when we are lazy and careless in handling His truth. He is grieved when we come before our people without having done the work necessary to say with as much confidence as a fallible and limited human being can say, "This is what God says, and this is what God means when He says it." Sloppy exegesis, careless sermon construction, and an unclear, disorganized presentation of the truth—these grieve the Holy Spirit. Should He come with present blessing and power on such ministerial delinquency and give His special assistance to the one engaging in it?

There is yet another way in which we can grieve the Holy Spirit and thereby experience a restrained or diminished measure of His present help in preaching. The Holy Spirit is grieved when there is an insufficient measure of preaching Christ in our sermonic endeavors. The Scriptures clearly teach us that in the accomplishment and the application of redemption, there is both oneness of will and purpose within the triune Godhead, and also a distinct function of redemptive activity by each of the persons within the Godhead. It is the Father who sends the Son. It is the Son who is sent and gives Himself as a ransom for sinners. It is the Holy Spirit who is sent by the Father and the Son to apply that salvation purposed by the Father and purchased by the Son.

The Holy Spirit does many distinctive things in the application of this redemption. Without being irreverent, let us imagine we have the privilege of asking the Holy Spirit this question: "Holy Spirit, what is Thy most delightful work in the application of the redemption purchased by the Son?" What do you think His answer would be? Would it not be that His most delightful work is that of shining on the face of Jesus, thereby making Him glorious to the hearts of sinners? To make the person and work of Christ understood, cherished, and believingly embraced in the hearts of men is indeed His delightful work. If this is so, then can we not envision the Holy Spirit hovering over our pulpits week by week in holy expectation as He anticipates doing His work of shining on the face of Christ? Can we not imagine Him saying to Himself, "Will I be able to do My most delightful work today through that man's preaching? Will the preacher give Me sufficient material with which to do My work? I have the lights all ready to turn on and focus on Jesus. Will the preacher put Christ front and center so that I can turn the floodlights of My influence on the Savior?" Or, is the Holy Spirit grieved because Jesus is not prominent in our preaching? Pierre Marcel makes the following striking statement: "The Holy Spirit is ardent to reveal the Christ."[1]

We must ask ourselves the following questions as we reflect on our preaching. "Where was the person and work of Christ in that sermon? Have I traced back to Christ, the source of all the grace and power for sufficiency to perform the duty, all the duties I have articulated? Have I drawn motives for obedience from our hearers' relationship to Christ? Have I traced back to Christ, who is the great fountainhead of all redemptive privilege, the privileges of grace I have expounded?" The Holy Spirit is grieved when our sermons are not full of Christ. We cannot expect the Holy Spirit to come with heightened measures of His agency and operation on us in our preaching when we grieve the Spirit, not only by laziness in our preparation and our ethical and moral controversies with God, but also in what we present as truth. When we move away from the nerve center of all truth, namely the person and work of the Lord Jesus, we grieve the Spirit of Christ. While it is nei-

---

1. Pierre Marcel, *The Relevance of Preaching* (Grand Rapids: Baker, 1977), 90.

ther biblical nor realistic to expect that Christ must be the explicit focus of every sermon we preach, it is biblical and realistic to expect that every sermon we preach will have something of the savor of the person and work of Christ.[2]

Quenching the Spirit

Third, the immediate agency and operation of the Spirit may be restrained or diminished because the Spirit is quenched by the preacher himself. Think of the incongruity of the situation. The man of God has gone to God, praying for and expecting the immediate agency and operation of the Holy Spirit in his preaching. However, in the very act of his preaching he violates the clear biblical injunction "quench not the Spirit" (1 Thess. 5:19). Consider the context of these words. They are followed by the commands, "despise not prophesyings" (5:20) and "prove all things" (5:21). These imperatives obviously deal with the exercise of public utterance gifts in the assembly of God's people. In his warning about quenching the Spirit, Paul uses a verb associated with quenching or extinguishing a fire. Paul plainly suggests that some operations of the Holy Spirit in conjunction with

---

2. "Pursuing a Ministry Permeated with Christ" (Oct 2005, MI-LL-1 and MI-LL-2) is a two-part message explaining this in more detail. It is also available from the Trinity Pulpit ministry of Trinity Baptist Church of Montville, New Jersey.

public utterance are like fire that can be dampened or quenched. Such operations of the Spirit are not to be snuffed out but given full latitude to burn in the pursuit of conveying God's truth. This line of reasoning leads us to the question, "How is the Spirit of God quenched in connection with a man's preaching?" If we are under a divine mandate—do not put out the fire of the Spirit—a mandate as clear as that in Ephesians 4:30, "do not grieve the Holy Spirit," then surely it is incumbent upon us to know in what way it is possible for us to quench the Spirit in the act of preaching. I offer the following as a partial answer to that concern.

We quench the Spirit when we refuse to make specific efforts to cultivate and improve our gift of preaching. The apostle Paul gives Timothy both a negative and a positive injunction in connection with this concern. In 1 Timothy 4:14 he writes, "Neglect not the gift that is in thee," the negative command. The positive injunction is given in 2 Timothy 1:6, where he commands Timothy to "stir up the gift of God." Again, Paul uses a verb that brings us into the category of fire. One could readily translate the text, "stir into flame"[3] the gift that is in you. On the

---

3. Frederick William Danker, Walter Bauer, William F. Arndt, and F. Wilbur Gingrich, eds., *A Greek-English Lexicon of the New Testament and Other Early Christian Literature*, 3rd ed. (Chicago: University of Chicago Press, 2001), s.v. *"anazopureo."*

surface of things, this seems to be a strange conjunction of ideas. Timothy is to recognize that his gift of utterance is a gift given to him by God. Yet the very gift given to him by God is that for which Timothy has responsibility for stirring into flame. By a deliberate and conscious effort in dependence on the Holy Spirit, Timothy is to embrace his responsibility to make specific efforts to cultivate and improve his gift of preaching. Failure to stir into flame the gift God has given us is, to some degree, an act of quenching the potential flame of the Spirit in conjunction with that gift.

Furthermore, the Spirit can be quenched by a carnal and slavish attachment to the labors of the study. Let me explain. I assume that under ordinary circumstances, each of us comes to the act of preaching accompanied by the results of our careful and prayerful preparation. How that preparation accompanies us into our pulpits will differ from one man to another. I deliberately avoid the question of how much paper should be produced in the study and carried with us into the pulpit. However, it is self-evident that no man should enter the pulpit, under ordinary circumstances, who does not bring with him the fruit of his arduous labors in the study.[4]

In addition, I assume that we have sought the

---

4. My pastoral theology lectures address this question with a good measure of historical perspective. They may be obtained

aid of the Spirit for our labors in the study and that we desire to share the fruit of those Spirit-assisted labors in our pulpits under a present assistance of the Holy Spirit. So far, so good, but now I assert something more. We ought to come to our pulpits with a prayerful expectation that, in the gathering of the people of God in the context of the promised special presence of Christ, Christ Himself will grant unplanned and unpredictable dimensions of His activity by the Spirit, which will require something other than a carnal and slavish attachment to the labors of the study, regardless of the form — manuscript, notes, memorized text — in which we bring the fruit of that study with us into the pulpit.

At this juncture I plead with the reader to give serious consideration to the following rather lengthy quotation from Pierre Marcel. It is taken from his aforementioned challenging little book. While I do not endorse everything in the book, I shall never forget the first time I read the following words. They acted like a bucket of cold ice water splashed on my face on a sultry summer day. They stunned me. They shocked me. For weeks afterward I carried this quotation folded over in the flyleaf of my Bible. During the offering and before the preaching I would read it. I would seek to have dealings with

---

from the Trinity Pulpit ministry of Trinity Baptist Church of Montville, New Jersey.

God concerning its contents. After giving some general directions concerning the necessity for pleading with God for the presence of the Holy Spirit in our worship, Marcel writes:

> But it is not enough to beseech the Spirit. He is not a diffuse force which spreads out in all directions as the heat of the sun and which can be channeled and annexed. The Spirit is a living and free person. It is necessary, therefore, when invoking his presence, to allow him freedom of action.
>
> This leads us to make a few ticklish remarks and to ask a few questions. How are the preacher and the believer going to depend upon the Holy Spirit and to leave to the Spirit of the Church his freedom in the very act of preaching?
>
> The Holy Spirit being the free Spirit of the Father and the Son, to what must the preacher's relationship with the Holy Spirit lead, since it is the Spirit who takes the things of the living Christ and communicates them to us? An attentive study of the commands and promises of Scripture and the practice of the apostles shows that during the preaching the preacher must depend directly on the living Christ, the living, speaking Word, the Church's permanent Teacher, who aids her with his Spirit. When we are called upon to bear witness, "do not be anxious how you are called upon to bear

witness; for what you are to say will be given you in that hour; for it is not you who speak, but the Spirit of your Father speaking through you" (Matt. 10:18–20).[5] An injunction and promise valid in all circumstances for every preacher! This does not, therefore, here mean an indirect dependence, a repetition of what Christ has already said during preparation and before the worship hour. Preparation and even redaction constitute only a preliminary part of preaching. It means rather that the preacher, in church, is to yield himself a malleable and living organ for what Christ by the Spirit wills him to say to those who hear. If Christ is left free, he will constrain the preacher to add, delete, and modify (in form or even in content) such and such portion of that which he had intended to say, but which he cannot now say. If the preacher is and remains dependent upon his manuscript or upon his memory, there is not just one prisoner — there are two: the preacher and the Spirit, and through the Spirit Christ. The written or memorized text of the sermon at this moment exercises its dominance; Christ

5. At this point Marcel gives an extended footnote answering objections to the use of this text as applicable to ordinary preachers. A summary of his footnote is this: "As for the promise in verse 20, it is corroborated in a general sense and is applicable to every preacher by numerous New Testament texts and by the experience of all those who in the ministry of preaching have taken it seriously."

through the Spirit is not free. To sound out the scriptures in the study, to prepare, to write, to reflect, to pray, on the one hand, and to preach, on the other, are distinct acts which employ the distinct and complementary interventions of the Spirit. One cannot replace the other."[6]

Interestingly, after making such a bold statement concerning this issue, Marcel immediately does what I have done throughout my treatment of this subject, namely, he hides behind Spurgeon. He cites the following thoughts from Spurgeon's book *The Greatest Fight in the World*:

In the pulpit do we really and truly rest upon the aid of the Spirit? I do not censure any brother for his mode of preaching, but I must confess that it seems very odd to me when a brother prays that the Holy Ghost may help him in preaching, and then I see him put his hand behind him and draw a manuscript out of his pocket, so fashioned that he can place it in the middle of his Bible, and read from it without being suspected of doing so. These precautions for ensuring secrecy look as though the man was a little ashamed of his paper; but I think he should be far more ashamed of his precautions. Does he expect the Spirit of God to bless him while he is practicing a trick?

6. Marcel, *The Relevance of Preaching*, 94–95.

And how can He help him when he reads out
of a paper from which anyone else might read
without the Spirit's aid? What has the Holy
Ghost to do with the business? Truly, He may
have had something to do with the manuscript
in the composing of it, but in the pulpit His
aid is superfluous. The truer thing would be to
thank the Holy Spirit for assistance rendered,
and ask that what He has enabled us to get
into our pockets may now enter the people's
hearts. Still, if the Holy Ghost should have
anything to say to the people that is not in the
paper, how can He say it by us? He seems to
me to be very effectually blocked as to fresh-
ness of utterance by that method of ministry.
Still, it is not for me to censure, although I
may quietly plead for liberty in prophesying,
and room for the Lord to give us in the same
hour what we shall speak.[7]

These assertions of Marcel and Spurgeon are not
fanatical and irresponsible. To avoid such a charge
I emphasize that these unexpected things that we
inject into our preaching should always be expressed
in a rational and self-controlled manner, even
though they were not in our notes or in our minds
when we entered the pulpit. In the living interaction
with the people of God in the presence of the living

7. Charles H. Spurgeon, *The Greatest Fight in the World*
(Pasadena, Tex.: Pilgrim Publications, 1999), 51–52.

Christ, a particular heading that in our preparation we thought we would cover in ten minutes, expands and ignites in the living current with our people. Additional applications may flood into our minds, but not out of nowhere. The things that come to us in such moments are rooted in the very truths over which we have labored in the study. However, there is an intensification and amplification of thought in the very birthing process of the sermon that causes the expansion of the material. While there may have been two specific and pointed applications to your people that came to your mind in the study, in the act of preaching three more may come to you. These applications grow out of your knowledge of your people, and you are therefore confident that they will be relevant to them.

On the other hand, as Marcel indicates, there may be things that powerfully gripped our minds and hearts in our preparation that, in the act of preaching, simply would seem irrelevant or counterproductive. We must be willing at that point in our preaching to omit such things as an act of faith. If we are so determined that our neat sermon will get preached out that we will not indulge such holy expansions, digressions, or omissions, we may well be quenching the Spirit. It is better to preach a ragged and less than neat sermon in the power of the Holy Spirit, than to preach a neat and polished sermon without His unction.

Why do we quench the Spirit with this carnal and slavish attachment to the labors of the study when we enter the pulpit? I suggest at least three reasons for this practice. The first is that we are in bondage to an excessive fear of saying something improper. We do not trust ourselves to get away from what we have hammered out in the study because we know that we are capable of saying things that are indeed imbalanced, imprecise, or downright inaccurate. Many times this is a good and noble caution. However, if this caution becomes a straitjacket to us, even when we have a sense of an expanded heart and mind in the act of preaching, then it may well be a chain binding us to a course of action in which we do indeed "quench the Spirit." If indeed we have done our proper work in the study, then we are not in the pulpit engaging in mindless chatter. Rather, we are talking about things concerning which we have been deeply exercised in heart and mind, which, in the act of preaching, are becoming amplified and expanded under the present ministry of the Holy Spirit. Does the Holy Spirit give us these things just to have them suppressed and swallowed so that the living Christ is not able to feed His sheep as He desires? Do not imprison the living Christ by an excessive fear of saying something improper or inaccurate!

There may well be times in those expanded patches when you will say something that subsequent sober reflection will make you regret. If so, you can always get up the next time you preach and acknowledge it by honest confession. I have made such a confession many times over the course of my forty-six years of pastoral ministry in one place and to one people. On the other hand, there is much that has helped God's people in a profoundly penetrating way that has come to their ears because I have been able in some measure to mortify the excessive fear of saying something improper.

In the second place, we often quench the Spirit by this carnal bondage to our preparation because of a lack of faith. We really doubt that the God who is giving the additional insight, the more penetrating analysis of the passage, and the more relevant and pointed or diffusive application, is giving these things to us for the benefit and edification of our hearers. This is nothing less than an expression of pulpit unbelief. While we are preaching, we must hear the words of the Lord Jesus ringing in our hearts again and again: "According to your faith be it unto you" (Matt. 9:29).

I come now to the third reason for this slavish adherence to the labors of the study as they are brought with us into the pulpit, which is unmortified pride in how we will look as preachers. We come into the pulpit with that which is homiletically neat and clean, and rightfully so. We are not paid to be sloppy and imprecise preachers serving up disorganized homiletical talk. However, as we begin to preach and we experience a fresh measure of the immediate assistance of the Holy Spirit in the act of preaching, the moment of truth comes. We know that if we follow the present impulses of the Spirit of God on our minds and hearts, we may well be destroying some element of the neatness of our previously prepared sermon. While you stand in the presence of God before your people you are confronted with the realization that to expand or reduce what was previously prepared will mean that the symmetry and organization of your sermon will be greatly disrupted.

This is the very point where we must be gripped with the passion and determination to "preach out" what the Spirit of God is giving us, rather than merely to "preach over" what was previously prepared. That may require some serious juggling of the material before the sermon is concluded. Many a time I have had to recompose on my feet, seeking to discover how I can go from the point of expansion to the conclusion of the sermon within a reasonable time frame. It may well be that it would be an expression of gross insensitivity to cover all of the prepared material. You may simply have to say, as I have done on many occasions, "Dear people, I do not know how to bring this to a neat and orderly conclusion. I simply don't have time to bring the other material I had prepared to set before you. I will end here. Let us pray." Be honest with your people. Forget your reputation as a neat homiletician. Go to a place called Golgotha and there behold your pride as an ugly manifestation of your old man which has been nailed to the cross in union with Christ. By all means, be Christ's free man. It is much better to preach a sermon that has the touch of the immediacy of the Spirit of God, even with its lack of neatness, than to preach an impeccably neat sermon without the peculiar unction of God on it.

CHAPTER 5

৵

Conclusion

As I bring this brief treatise to a conclusion, I trust the reader has been challenged with respect to this whole matter of the immediate agency and operation of the Holy Spirit in and on the preacher in the act of preaching. Where this aspect of the Holy Spirit's ministry has been ignored or despised, I trust there will be deep and thorough repentance for the sins associated with quenching the Holy Spirit. For others who have had an intellectual consciousness of these realities but who have experienced a restraining or withdrawal of them in their own ministry, may there again be deep and thorough repentance touching anything and everything that has grieved the Holy Spirit. For some of my readers, honest dealings with God and men may well demand a frank and open confession of sin to one's congregation, since they have suffered because of one's grieving or quenching the Holy Spirit in connection with preaching.

For others who have ignored these aspects of the Spirit's activity, beginning to acknowledge both the necessity and desirability of the Spirit's agency and operation in preaching should lead to new dimensions of earnest prayer and expectancy for His ministry in their preaching. To those who do so pray, God's gracious answer may become so evident in their preaching that their hearers will be tempted to believe that there is indeed such a thing as a "second work of grace"!

Others of you who have been grieving the Holy Spirit, and in whom there has been a diminishing of His present and powerful activity in your preaching, if you repent and begin seeking a fresh empowering of the Spirit, it will be evident to your people that the dew of heaven is once more resting on your pulpit labors. They will no longer need to excuse, in the love that "bears all things," the obvious waning of spiritual power in your preaching.

For those of you who have had an inaccurate view of the relationship between the labor of the study and the labor of the pulpit, I trust your thinking has been challenged and that you are now convinced that you may possibly be trying to preach Christ while imprisoning Christ in your notes, your manuscript, or your memorized text. Let Christ loose so that He may stand among the gathered people of God and exercise His role as the great Prophet of the church.

Many are now telling us that in this postmodern age, preaching is passé. We are being told that "one-way authoritative proclamation of truth" is totally incompatible with the mindset of Generation Xers, baby boomers, and those who have bought into the mindset of postmodernism. However, I am still convinced that preachers who stand before men with minds and hearts aglow with the truth, men liberated and empowered by the Spirit, so that what they preach throbs and sings with heavenly life, light, and music—these men will be heard. God has chosen preaching as His grand weapon to dismantle the kingdom of darkness and to establish the kingdom of His dear Son. But not just any kind of preaching will serve. God's grand weapon is preaching with the presence and powerful agency and operation of the Holy Spirit. He regards this sword as David did Goliath's: "There is none like that; give it me" (1 Sam. 21:9). May God, by His grace, be pleased to make us such instruments of grace to our needy generation.